D0689561

PROTECTION SPELL

2017 finalist
MILLER WILLIAMS
poetry prize

Givhan, Jennifer,
Protection spell :
poems /
2017.
33305237094010
mi   05/11/17

PROTECTION SPELL

POEMS BY JENNIFER GIVHAN

The University of Arkansas Press
Fayetteville
2017

Copyright © 2017 by The University of Arkansas Press
All rights reserved
Manufactured in the United States of America
ISBN: 978-1-68226-028-9
e-ISBN: 978-1-61075-610-5

21   20   19   18   17   5   4   3   2   1

Designed by Liz Lester

⊗ The paper used in this publication meets
the minimum requirements of the American National Standard
for Permanence of Paper for Printed Library Materials Z39.48-1984.

Library of Congress Control Number: 2016956683

for Jeremiah and Adelina
and our communities that thrive
like flowers on cacti, rising
from the crags of desert rock.

But here is my pain that is neither a father nor a son. It hasn't any back to get dark, and it has too bold a front for dawning, and if they put it into some dark room, it wouldn't give light, and if they put it into some brightly lit room, it wouldn't cast a shadow.

—CÉSAR VALLEJO *(trans. Robert Bly)*

SERIES EDITOR'S PREFACE

Miller Williams was the first editor to spot me, you might say, and subsequently, the one who published my first full-length book of poems, *The Apple That Astonished Paris,* in 1988. With a single stroke, I was transformed into a "published poet," an all-too-common phrase that reminds us of the vast number of poets who are unpublished, or as an optimist might say, "pre-published." Funny, we don't hear much about "unpublished novelists" or "unpublished journalists."

Since then, I have felt a special debt to Miller for the validation he gave me and for the delicacy with which he edited that collection. "You have a line that goes, 'I can see it so clearly.' I don't think you need that intensifier '*so*,'" he told me in our first talk on the phone. I was left with the feeling that this man had read my poems more closely and carefully than I had. I won't forget that initial phone call. Miller happened to find me in a hotel in Miami, where I was getting dressed to go to Hialeah for a day at the races. When I heard him say he was going to publish my book, I knew I'd been granted more than enough luck for one day; it was a pleasure to spend the afternoon losing one race after another. I wasn't just someone who couldn't pick a winner; I was a *published poet* who couldn't pick a winner. The day was made even better because my best pal was with me, and we even ran into Carol Flake, whose horse book, *Tarnished Crown,* was just about to be published.

Judging this prize, which is named in honor of the cofounder and director of the University of Arkansas Press, gives me the opportunity to pass on the gift that Miller Williams gave to me, the publication of a book of poems, in some cases a first book. For a poet, in terms of sheer thrills, there is no publication that matches his or her first book. With all this in mind, it follows that serving as judge for the Miller Williams Poetry Prize is great pleasure for me.

Even if one is so blissfully egalitarian and nonjudgmental as to believe that all poetry manuscripts are equal, one must concede that some are more equal than others. This year, all of the "more equal" ones were eye-openers for me, literary wake-up calls that brought me to attention, each for a very different reason.

Self-Portrait in a Door-Length Mirror might be an intentional echo of Ashbery's convex mirror, but Stephen Gibson's language is neither coy nor elliptical as Ashbery's typically is. Instead, Gibson presents a series of clear formalist poems, each organized around a different kind of patterning. A series of 8 seven-line poems—each in the rectangular shape of a painting—examines the life and art of Pierre Bonnard. But the focus is Marthe de Méligny, Bonnard's lover, model, and eventually, his wife. The eroticism of Marthe washing her feet in a bathtub or being submerged in it naked is balanced by the mention of the objects in the painting where "everything alive . . . is dead." Add to this grouping an intricately successful pantoum about Diane Arbus, along with my favorite, a twenty-seven-line monorhyme (a tour de force, by the way) written in reaction to a photograph of Hermann Göring's suicide. The radical subjects of Arbus (also a suicide) and SS Commander Göring are brought under control by the imposition of form. The resulting tension shows this exceptional poet at his rhyming best.

Mr. Stevens' Secretary—yes, it's *that* Mr. Stevens—is a series of vignettes taken from (or invented to create) the life of the great modernist's secretary. We see what Stevens looked like from her point of view, which includes how Stevens smelled—not bad as it turns out: "Oriental . . . but that may be that was because of the tea . . . White peony tea." A mild eroticism builds when we are told that the secretary keeps a special bottle of Chantilly "not at home but in her desk." We also get to see the secretary outside of her job in a poem about wasps and marriage and another about her pre-Stevens employers. But it is the famous poet who cannot distinguish *its* from *it's*. In another poem, she attempts to write a fable in which a father saves a cat who got its head stuck in a milk bottle, yet he has an awful temper and shouts "horribly" at his wife. Like Carol Ann Duffy's boldly feminist collection, *The World's Wife,* Frances Schenkkan's *Mr. Stevens' Secretary* forces readers to adjust their perspective by showing a great man through the eyes of a previously silent and less visible woman.

One requirement for poets is the ability to write about two different things at the same time. Seamus Heaney turns writing into a kind of digging. John Ciardi intertwines marriage and the structure of an arch. Among the several poems in Jennifer Givhan's *Protection Spell* that stopped me cold is "The Polar Bear," in which a mother tries to protect her black child from the television news of racial unrest (riots, arrests, brutality) by turning his attention to the Discovery Channel. But there, a polar bear is fighting for survival surrounded by vicious walruses and melting ice. The boy clutches his stuffed white bear and asks if this is real. Life in the Arctic and life in the urban streets are conjoined, ecology and racism wed. Givhan is a poet of great heart and brave directness who writes real-life poems, sometimes crowded to the point of claustrophobia with the details of life in the poor lane. One poem transforms a laundromat woman living "paycheck to paycheck" into a "god." Another poem is a stirring defense of cheerleaders, written without a drop of irony. A reader will be quick to trust the authority in this poet's voice and the credentials of experience that are on full display.

Not all the poems in *The Wild Night Dress* by Laura McCullough use scientific or technological language, but many of them do, and in ways that create interesting effects. This poet has the kind of binocular vision that can see the poetic and scientific aspects of the world simultaneously. The poem "Feed" opens: "In a drone video of Humpbacks / feeding off the coast of Canada, / the surface of the ocean is frothed into blossoms." The ending of that last line returns the poem to poetry's musical origins without implying any friction between this lovely sound and drone technology. In a poem in which the speaker hungers for eggs, this mix of diction occurs: "though I wish to fill myself, / until the ventro-medial hypothalamus [the gland that stimulates hunger] / is so stimulated / all I can think of is flowers." This shuffling together of lyrical/botanical and medical language is done so gracefully, it has the effect of bringing "the two cultures" into a rare state of peaceful coexistence. Also engaging are the more traditionally lyric poems, one about childhood, another about a "fawn caught in the family compost" (for me, an echo of the cat caught in a milk bottle in *Mr. Stevens' Secretary*), but the distinction this collection can best claim is the way the poems find an easy synthesis between poetry and science. Perhaps Laura McCullough's most telling confession lies in this couplet: "I can't help loving / the word *sonoluminescence.*"

I'm glad that early on, the editors at the press and I agreed that the judge for these prizes should not be looking for poems that sound like the poems of Miller Williams but for poems that Miller might have enjoyed and admired. It's easy for me to picture Miller paging through these four books with a look of appreciation and even delight on his face, though he might keep a red pencil nearby just in case he comes across one of those annoying, unnecessary "intensifiers."

Billy Collins

x

ACKNOWLEDGMENTS

My deep gratitude to the journals in which these poems first appeared, sometimes in different form:

Acentos Review: "Prayer." *Adroit*: "In the Emergency Room." *Blueshift*: "Ars Poetica after Baby Lyuba." *Boston Quarterly*: "The Empathy Machine." *Brooklyn Quarterly*: "The Empathy Machine." *Crazyhorse*: "The Accusation." *Connotation Press*: "First Light in Tahoe City" and "Reverse: Ten Years of Marriage." *Crab Creek Review*: "Santiago's Song" and "In the Beginning" (Finalists 2015 Poetry Prize). *Cultural Weekly*: "In the Shower with Sunday after Watching *Lost*," "Machine for Second Chances." *Indiana Review*: "My God, Nieve" (Runner-up 2015 Poetry Prize). *Indianola Review*: "Reupholstering a Chair." *Kenyon Review*: "Race in America." *Kweli Journal*: "English 20: Developmental Writing." *Lascaux Review*: "The Polar Bear" (2015 Poetry Prize Editors' Choice winner, republished). *Life and Legends*: "Prayer Remix." *Malpais Review*: "Safe: One Boy." *Michigan Quarterly Review*: "Volver (Bride Price)" and "Fernweh (At Gorge Bridge, Taos NM)." *PANK*: "Abiyoyo." *Passages North*: "The Trial" (finalist 2016 Neutrino Short-Short Prize). *Prairie Schooner*: "Carrying Baby." *Rattle*: "The Glance" (Finalist 2015 Poetry Prize), "The Cheerleaders," "An Editor Advised Me to Stop Writing Mother Bird Poems" and "The Polar Bear" (Poets Respond). *Reservoir*: "Inca Ice Maiden." *Rose Red Review*: "Manju Speaks." *Saranac Review*: "The Perennials" (nominated for Pushcart Prize 2015). *Scissors and Spackle*: "Cemetery Nights." *Southern Humanities Review*: "Protection Spell (Riot's

Eye)" (Finalist 2015 Auburn Witness Prize). *Sugar House Review*: "Elegy, for Sunday." *Superstition Review*: "Junkyard Halflight." *TriQuarterly*: "Snakes-Her-Skirts." *Vinyl*: "The Problem with My Eyes." *Witness*: "Curanderisma." *200 New Mexico Poems Centennial Anthology*: "Mrs. Francis Na Kai at the Birthday Party." *32 Poems*: "Earth" and "Sunday Night Shift." Some of these poems also appeared in the chapbooks *Curanderisma* (Dancing Girl Press) and *Lifeline* (Glass Poetry Press).

I'm thankful to the NEA for the fellowship that made writing this book possible. The Community of Writers at Squaw Valley and to The Frost Place, where some of these poems first began to grow. Faithful readers and friends, Alicia Elkort, Stephanie Bryant Anderson, Avra Elliott, Stacey Balkun, Molly Sutton Kiefer. All my Candle Poets and our 30/30s. Mentor Van Jordan, who pushed me to transcend. Billy Collins and the University of Arkansas Press and the wonderful editors of the Miller Williams Poetry Series. My family, Paul, David, Grandma Linda and Grandpa Rafael Casas, Grandma Marge. Mom and Dad, for bringing Taco Tuesdays so I could fight the good fight. My children, J. and A., for whom I write. My son's birthmother. Andrew, for everything else.

CONTENTS

PROTECTION SPELL

My God, Nieve

My god at the laundromat says her washing machine works
but the power's out so she's been drying it by line. My god

waits in line at the WIC counter to weigh her kids, account
for their eating habits, check the box for *no*

they're not eating mud or lead or other poisons
and *yes* she gets it: her choices are dry or canned beans

or peanut butter. My god's not allergic to peanut butter, likes
the creaminess gumming her bread-mouth,

her ten-dollars-worth of fresh *or* frozen veggie coupons.
On a dare, at fourteen, my god stole a carton

of Thrifty's Rocky Road, tried convincing the store manager
she was pregnant under her Sally-dress, but got so cold,

my god, she dropped the box right there in the aisle,
grateful she got caught. Now the cashier pays my god

veggie change in cash, so she buys each kid a cone. My god
is frozen-mouth. She is get-out-of-this-town-

or-hell-freezes-over. She is paycheck
to paycheck. Each night when she goes to bed, my god

kisses her kids' clean faces, then, thanking herself, her own.

The Polar Bear

I'm just another asshole sitting behind a desk writing about this
—Facebook status update

What I'm asking is will watching the Discovery
Channel with my young black boy instead
of the news coverage of the riot funerals riot arrests
riot nothing changes riots be enough to keep him
from harm? We are on my bed crying for what we've done
to the polar bears, the male we've bonded with on-screen
whose search for seals on the melting ice has led him
to an island of walruses and he is desperate, it is late-
summer and he is starving and soon the freeze
will drive all life back into hiding, so he goes for it,
the dangerous hunt, the canine-sharp tusks
and armored hides for shields, the fused weapon
they create en masse, the whole island a system
for the elephant-large walruses who, in fear, huddle
together, who, in fear, fight back. This is not an analogy.
The polar bear is hungry. The walruses fight back.
A mother pushes her pup into the icy water
and spears the hunter through the legs, the gut,
his blood clotting his fur as he curls into the ice
only feet away from the fray—where the walruses
have gathered again, sensing the threat has passed.
My boy's holding his stuffed animal, the white body
of the bear he loves, who will die tonight (who
has already died) and my boy asks me
is this real? What I'm asking is how long will we stay
walruses, he and I, though I know this is not an analogy.

Protection Spell (Riot's Eye)

They're chasing my boy, his
dreadlocks streaming

behind him like bed sheets
from the second-story

window of a house fire.

       He and the asphalt
dovetail

I watch and I watch
like a black hole swallowing

a baby universe. (This is the last
of the gunmetal dreams.)

I wring the blood
from my ribcage

my world in your chest, child.

       When I was a child
I believed God held us

like a paper bag
to the mouth of a panic attack.

       How I'm holding
a city like my boy,

my boy to my own
siren wail—

How the wind-as-breath
            moved us, bent our

tallest trees
to snapping, like our songs

on our knees.

Race in America

i. Domestic Adoption:

No joke, black babies are cheaper—
white ones cost ten grand more. That's not
how she phrased it, on the phone
after the gauge of my uterus
had fixed itself on empty.

I'd made peace with the threat of
you're not my "real" mother and
called for information, but here's
how it broke down:
30k service fees for white babies,
20k for black. *The waitlist is shorter*
she told me. *Most of our couples want babies*
who look like them.

Imagine her joy when she found out *we* were
a biracial couple, Sunday and me, and we *were* looking
for a black baby. Imagine how we took
out loans cosigned with my mother
and how the call came just two months later,
faster than any other couple there.

ii. Strolling through Koreatown

> new home where we'd sought peace after
> death threats posted on our apartment door:

We watch the garbage truck lift its steely arms
and heave our trash bin over its shoulders.

The garbage man honks his horn.
Mack! you yell. You think all trucks are called that.

A grandfather trundles his grandson-
filled cart toward our neighborhood market.

Fish fry in the air, fire-bright koi in the pond.
I don't need to convince you we're *safe*.

You grin and say *Hi!* He nods.
The other baby stares but says nothing.

You peel the tan bark off a birch tree like a scab,
thumb it, inspect it: *Nice tree.*

iii. Rainstorm (after the riots):

The child believes

he is made only

of glass

until it rains

and the child

walks the streets

umbrella-less

only then

he can create,

with his

body   a prism

splitting

light

I might never

have seen.

Prayer

When I lost you at the market, I cleared
each shelf for your folded little boy body

(what was it you loved in hide and seek?
the brief escape, the minutes you didn't belong

to me, when no one could find you until)
I found you with a muumuu'd woman

hunkered between shopping carts. You'd gifted
her your animal crackers for offering you

a prayer. My son, performing miracles
every time you wash your feet or clean your

plate of fish sticks, my heart cliff-dives
when I find you weeping for a classmate

or alone in the yard watching a cloud
rising from the river, so when I grabbed your

little body, hugged you, took in your scent
of sweat and cookies and dirt, I swore I'd

never lose you again. My cheeks hot
against yours, I wondered if you knew my

only prayer, whispered nightly: *God, if you
ask me to let him go, I'll say* fuck no.

The Glance

for Sunday

Through window through curtains wide through
singing after shower through racial lines and statutory
laws through landscape pebbles off the complex
path through morning's rituals before the sun could rise
through glass pane while I dreamt in our bed while our
plump brown baby slept in his slatted crib through slanted
white light through window on your way to work you heard
a song you heard a sweet song and turned your head toward
the naked girl. When the police knocked on our door.
When the police came to our door. Let me rephrase
that. When the police. They claimed you climbed
on a rock. They claimed it was a shower, the white
girl's white mother. They claimed the window
was the shower's and the window eight feet high.
They claimed you carried ladders or were made of stilts
or could form pebbles into whole rocks for climbing.
They made signs they posted on our door.
They made signs for better watch our backs.
They made signs for night watch for on guard
for dark man with Afro. After we'd moved away
after we'd hired a lawyer and the case was dropped
for lack of evidence after there was no rock
after we'd claimed the jagged edges of any safe space
we could, in Koreatown, where I daily pushed
our baby's stroller through the apartment's garden
with koi ponds past doorways that smelled of boiled
fish and our baby learned to name the things he saw

nice tree the oak with gall, the spindle wasp gall that leaves
had formed like scar tissue around the wound
where insect larva were eating their way through
the window of a neighbor's home I looked up
and watched a round man from the shower, letting
towel slip I couldn't look away from this strange
intoxicating body in front of me. We know
nothing happened after that. I took our boy
home. I cooked us all dinner. We shut the blinds.

Mrs. Bitterstout

Before sunrise I go downhill
for coffee, streetlight quietly wrestling starfade
in the parking lot, an image, splitting—
a twin sent away at birth.

Did she change her name when she had the chance?
I didn't take it. Years before,
that first week I was married, barely old enough
to drink legally, Sunday and I at the bar

tried conjuring names for ourselves. I wanted
us to share, but I didn't want his.
It hadn't served him well, a junkwatch his dead-
so-no-longer-deadbeat father had left him,

replete with an absurd junior at the end
though he was the third son. *How about Paloma
or Mojito?* I asked. I still wish Mama hadn't taken
my dad's gringo name and kept her own, which

I could've felt at-home in. He laughed, opening
his throat for the rest of his beer. *In
that case, Bitterstout.* I slugged his shoulder, feeling
already too young and sober to be that free

and trapped at once. We could've been Mr. and
Mrs. Football's-Playing-And-We-Don't-Care,

or the Pretzelbasket couple, or
the Met-And-Married-In-Six-Months'es.

Instead I went to the social security office,
stripped myself of childhood and dressed
in his old name, wearing it snugly.
Now I want to ask *Who are you, strange sister, buying*

a cranberry-orange scone and stealing
the window seat? I don't want to disturb her,
reflection in the glass, but I can't resist
telling her what darkness will come, what light.

The Problem with My Eyes

in memory of Sophia O'Neill

is that what they see
burns imprints in the light

so when I close them there are shadows
the shapes of what I cannot lid

and when the sky is bright as blood with first morning light
this is not a problem

the way I look up toward the mountain's curved spine
the jagged rocks pinned with firs

and the background swims with light
I mean it teems with it, for the swirling

of my eyes, for the blurring they create—
but when I see you, child, still

crushed beneath your mother's boyfriend's boot
the problem is I need to know what light you saw

before you swam toward what must have been a sandbank
a spidering web a trapeze net

or was it blurred or was it rocks or was it me
who never knew you but would have loved—

child against that shadow, I carry you.

The Perennials

Again, this reddening:
we dig for miracles

in our crematorial
plots, bedding thorned

rosehips, forget-me-nots.
But we can't unbury

our blanketed boys,
soiled girls, our mirror-

images welling earth
sick-drunk

with consistency,
our trying to make

annuals out of ashes.
What could weeding bring us

but sweating something besides
redemption, and drained.

English 20: Developmental Writing

. . . ay, es para mi sobrinito.
A paper-wrapper coffer box for her

sister's baby rests on the desk, somber gift
with a single photo taped to the side.

Pobrecito died before his first birthday.
She's taking a collection

(even a miniature coffin costs too much).
After class, she asks for change

from her classmates and me, her teacher.
I fumble through my wallet

but find no bills, no coins, and apologize,
hoping she knows I don't mean about the money.

I can't tell her I came to campus today
bleeding my positive pregnancy test onto a pad.

She holds my gaze.
Maybe she doesn't believe me about the change

but hears the heaviness in my voice.
Está bien. There's no lesson here.

Paucity. We breathe.
Brevity. We swallow.

My students understand these words
beyond their meanings, hobbling along.

English is her second language.
I hear loss in her first.

Carrying Baby

On an airplane, Lucy ate her cheese baby
and in this, my favorite episode, before
she squirrels her cheeks with it, she burps the hulking
cheese, slick and stinking in a blanket. I'm carrying
loads of baby wannabes like unpopped caviar
strung to my cauliflower ovaries, dreading
at what junction I'll need to stop and rethink this
burden, at which exit I'll let go. An Amish woman
on the train from Albuquerque to Chicago, traveling
with kin to a convention, bundled a perfect-painted baby
doll, honey-colored eyelashes and baby hair
curled around her porcelain face. At nightfall, she rocked
and sang her to sleep, like Amish girls who wrap
rags around logs, pretending they're dolls. Only this one
had a face, perhaps to prove something to the eyes
of God. Beneath the woman's white bonnet
her drape-heavy black dress, her smell of sweat,
body odor thick as stockings in the dank coach car
she carried an ache, ripping at the crisp edges.

The Cheerleaders

If you have not written your cheerleader poem,
they're good for many things—

The Writers' Conference

I want to defend the cheerleaders
to those who've said it was anti-feminist
here at the mountain camp

in the Sierra Nevadas among the Jeffrey pine
with its bark that smells of vanilla and
the same Bailey's Irish Cream I first tasted

in high school, at a party—
these girls are rural and white, too young
for sex to be sexualized, bright pink

blooming bows in their hair, tightly coiled
with immaculate white woven through
their chanting as if in ecstasy

everything, here among the white-
flowered cat paws that lay close to the ground
each cold summer night then rise

toward the sun come noon, the cheerleaders
shout for themselves, but at home,
for the team, for the boys, toward

the moon—the way I was a cheerleader
in the Southwestern desert twenty minutes
from the Mexicali border in the egg-

frying summer heat, and my boyfriend
after spooning me all day in the guest bed
at his nana's would drive me to practice—

I'd fit my thick thighs into lycra-tight shorts,
pull taut my dark hair and bother anyway with bronze
Covergirl foundation and glittered purple eyeliner

though I'd sweat it all off in an hour
of basing basket tosses, of being the one to lift
another girl freer than me, the one who kept

flying girls from falling to packed-earth, scorched
dirt below our white and silver gel-inspired
ASICS training shoes with flexible soles for dancing—

but one girl flew to the left of our interlocked
crisscrossed arm basket and we couldn't catch her
before she landed on her side, on her chest, palms

down but she didn't break any bone
or the baby we found three weeks later
sprouting like a flower beneath her bruised ribcage.

I want to defend these girls in the tall grass
with their backs to the lake with their black
and red skirts like fringed ballet tutus

or costume burlesque, their cheer faces
like masks I'd put on and practice
when my mother asked why I was moody

and what were the bruises purpling my arms
my hips my thighs. What's not feminist
about this, how the sport could send us—

most of whom had never been on a plane
since there was no airport in our town
besides barns for crop dusters—

to New York City. It's not recklessness or
drunkenness but the culture, its lack
of options, how I wanted to dance

where there were no dance schools
where the only art was sprayed on the bellies
of walls where resistance meant

disobeying our parents meant breaking
curfew meant bonfires in barrels
meant sex between sweet-smelling stacks

of alfalfa beside hay bales beside ditchwater.
I want to defend these cheerleaders
in their sassy and hopeful irreverent poses

how Nietzsche says metaphor is desire
to be somewhere else, how the cheerleaders
are likewise, the pouty lips they taught us

openly mocked, the meanest of us
the toughest the loudest to cheer
remind me still of the pinecones that'll stay

closed with pitch until hit with fire
then open, that need damage, some seeds
need a bit of abuse before they can germinate

like forest freeze, like fire, an animal's gut,
these serotinous cones that the lodgepole pine
give of themselves to be hurt—like the cheerleaders

of my girlhood, of the *go!* of the *big blue!*—
they aren't thinking of this or of anything
as they lift toward the sky and take root.

Cemetery Nights

after Stephen Dobyns

The dead line up in the schoolyard for dodgeball. The dead haven't heard that dodgeball is now illegal as bathroom screwing. I am one of the dead sometimes, and when I am dead, I spider myself backwards like slumber party twister like double dog dare or ditch-dial ringing that cord spiraling around another dead girl's neck like umbilical instead of dodging I swallowed instead of living I curled into a seashell or the ocean inside I know now is only echoing the surrounding chaos and trunked belly, lime-green fetal limbs like poison wolf lichen rattling like beetles in the reeds and we were way too young for that sick shit. The dead leave marks on each other too. A girl's wild bright flame from the tall grasses—bruises thrilling my skin.

The Trial

for Sunday

I was dancing in a Richard Simmons video
while you were in court. They let me bring
him to the studio, our baby whose curly
hair matched the aerobic instructor's. I'd been
infertile and lost fifty pounds to stress and
though everyone kept telling me how healthy
I looked, I wanted to tell them I was starving,
how even strings of chicken breast turned
to wires scratching at my throat like nooses
though I know this is the 21*st* century
and we're beyond those times of killing
mockingbirds in public lynchings.
The day you lost your job (you got it back)
was the day Michael Jackson died. I'd just heard
on the news, our baby on my hip in the living
room of that Koreatown apartment, wooden
spoon for the red rice in my hand, my face
splotchy from crying and the baby
not understanding but singing along
in his baby words *lookin' through the windows*
and Michael in that orange jumpsuit as a boy
on Sonny and Cher with The Jackson Five
saying *I can't decide what I'll be when I grow up—*
a jet pilot, an astronaut, or the governor of Georgia,
how I held him tighter, fighting fear our world
would end (earthquake, swine flu, police

knocking at the door) when you walked in shaking
midday. You kept apologizing. Like you'd done
something wrong. We got WIC
'cause my adjunct job didn't pay shit
and I held my head high at grocery registers
when the cashiers sneered at me and double-
checked my math. We moved in with my mom
who invited me to drive the thirty miles
through Los Angeles traffic to Beverly Hills
for Saturday morning dance class with Richard
to boogie down the pounds. But really,
she said, to save my life. I wasn't eating and
Richard was all about recovery, those pre-dance
circle chats on the spongy wooden floor, disco
ball above us, we'd talk eating disorders
and loving ourselves, I mean, really loving
ourselves. Richard had lost his hair
to anorexia and the curls were plugs,
our boy in the corner sucking his fists.
What are you going to be when you grow up?
Richard asked him. I wanted to say
He can be anything and still end up
at the courthouse like his daddy
but I was shimmying with the spandex-
neon tagalongs who'd come to poke their fun,
the hipster gentrifiers stepping on my feet

or the plus-sized men and women who needed
a savior like we did—I was chicken,
love. I got you a lawyer nothing like Atticus
and took our baby to nothing like Gymboree.
The producers came to the studio and
it was cheer squad again, another
out. I'm not asking for forgiveness.
The way I didn't believe you at first
the way trauma works—
in the medical field the term is
"second victim." When the caregiver
fucks up and injects
potassium chloride into the IV drip
instead of plain old saltwater—
stops the heart. How for years
the nurse will revisit that night in the dark
and turn on the fucking light
and read the label on the bag of liquid death.
What else could I have done
but sided with the girl whose body
shamed her into silence? I mean, my body.
I mean, I know now there was no body.
See what I mean? It's hard to tell sometimes
the smell of chicken boiling in a pot
on the stove in our small world where news

of the outside came like birdsong over
the wall A/C and the neighbors
below never knew we were threatened
with death when we moved in quietly
and kept to ourselves, to our small days
beside the manicured lawns
and stocked koi ponds. Those fish.
They terrified me sometimes.
The way they burned in the water.
But I'd lost enough weight that my body
stopped breaking—or a miracle
in my otherwise sac of sulfuric eggs
because the pee test turned pink twice
and I loved to joke that Richard Simmons
got me pregnant. Even you laughed at that.

The Empathy Machine

The spider I killed first
    (I feared it might hurt us)—

then the fly on the window
(its broken-clock sound). I peeled it

from glass with an envelope's back
and watched its red eyes bulge

its body already paper-stiff,
wings like butcher's wrap, rainbow-tinged

threaded mildew-green at the edges.
I studied it while the warm-blooded dog

sniffed and whined at my hand
then followed me to the bathroom

where I flushed My Noiseless One
    —My Moral Relative.

I've heard of children dropping
small animals

from rooftops onto trampolines
stories below. I've heard there were no

survivors. I've heard without exhaling
the clinking of copper pennies we lay

on each other's eyes—
          I've heard across the river
(like dog paws on tile)

water lapping boat.
—The buzzing of the coils that bear us

together. The crackling
of wires. (I'm guilty of more

than I admit.) Climb with me
up some great height. Dare us not to fall.

Prayer Remix

for runaways, for aphonic choirs, for vinegar
flies in tangerines. Prayer for hassling into
lingerie a size too small, for pinching elastic thighs.

Prayer for the suicide, the chronic angel, restless
spirit of toxic nights. Prayer for rivers
flowing with waste. For bees in their cases

of thirst. Prayer because I've forgotten
how to pray. Because the hymn says I'll praise
in darkness, because I'm afraid. Prayer for monsters

masquerading as love. For bodies. For tongues
like guns. Prayer for commandments and the strange
prayer gods. Prayer for two or more gathered

in prayer, for shuteye, for danger, for rust. Yes,
prayer for the rust in the back of the throat
for praying, for mouths, for crusted with hope.

Half Mexican

Whenever I start writing about identity I start doubting why I matter.

My husband was stopped on his way home from work. He was wearing his maroon nursing scrubs and hospital badge. The officer said he *fit a description*, held him on the side of the road for hours, called the nursing home where he dresses wounds to check his story. They were looking for a thug.

There's always something that matters more than what I'm doing.

I'm not compiling a list of microaggressions. I'm not even telling you my story.

o

Identity is slippery. My husband says what if people think I'm not *valid*, not really Latin@ because I'm half white. He's half black. He can say things like this. Or he's trying to make a point, playing devil's advocate. His words ricochet in my mind all week. I light candles at the altar I've made above my bed, in the window facing the Sandia Mountains, Spanish for watermelon, their pink glow at sunset. The candles drip wax down my wall, red-orange smudging whitewash, that stark paint.

Earlier in the day he took a sage smudge stick and burned it across our doorways, our walls.

I didn't choke on the smoke.

○

I explain to my white father why being Latin@ matters to me.

He's not arguing with me, sitting on the couch with a bag of Cocoa Puffs he's eating by the handful like chips or peanuts, a golf tournament on television. He's listening, crunch crunch, as I expound identity theory and erasure of the artist, crunch crunch, how *the author is dead* was born as women and minorities began publishing what they'd been hiding in closets, crunch crunch. He doesn't get it, but he's listening.

There was a time he and his dad used to say racist shit about Tiger Woods.

They've changed since I married my husband. They didn't just stop repeating the jokes, I mean, they even stopped thinking they were funny.

○

I share ancestry with Frida Kahlo: half Mexican half German. In fifth grade I took Mama's razor and shaved my legs, dry. I didn't know about soap and water, so I have a scar down my left shin. Mama told me she would've helped me if I'd told her why—my armpits too, my arms, my eyebrows. I plucked them into thatched rooftops, stark angles above my dark eyes.

Now I have nine Fridas on my walls, not including the doll Avra made me. None of them smiles.

○

My dad drove a beige jalopy, picked me up from Sacred Heart every afternoon. The rich white kids laughed. They were *all* rich, the white kids. Children of farmers in our border town. We were there on scholarship.

My brother is full Mexican. I don't know if he feels different than I do or not. I've never asked him.

He grew up with our father too. But our father called him things like *your kid*, meaning Mama's, and *sissy boy* or *fag*. I hated our father too sometimes, when he said those things.

When my brother came out to his own father, on a fishing trip, when they were both grownups, his dad hugged him, said he loved him as boat lapped ocean. I wasn't there. I'm imagining the details.

○

We watched musicals every weekend, Mama, my brother, and I. Seven Brides for Seven Brothers, Hello Dolly, The Unsinkable Molly Brown, Singing in the Rain, Oklahoma, Carousel. We sang all the songs.

○

I don't know if I can say that the Mexican kids never accepted me because I didn't speak Spanish. The white ones never understood our arroz con pollo, fighting for the burnt at the bottom of the pot, our tres leches and tortillas instead of bread. But that's a lie. They liked our food. They'd order it from Nana Dora's, their stay-at-home moms would deliver it to them at lunchtime. I ate cafeteria food.

When I was eleven the white kids dared me to eat a whole jalapeño; since I was Mexican, they said, it wouldn't sting.

My mom is full Mexican. She doesn't eat chile or jalapeños or salsa because of her ulcer.

Also, she has nothing to prove.

○

I'm not ashamed of my white father. Not anymore. I was never ashamed of him for being white.

Maybe for being poor. For wearing nothing but underwear when he got up in the mornings and went into the kitchen for his instant Folgers coffee crystals, or nothing but shorts (no shirt) when he was watering the front yard, baring his gleaming pale and hairy chest.

But I never much noticed he was white.

Not even at the dinner table when Mama or abuela or anyone else would talk about those gringos locos.

o

Ice rain. Sleet. There was frozen water pouring all night into early morning when the police came to our door.

The welcome mat slippery, there are things we've endured.

Resfeber (Re-Membering Trauma)

The nervous feeling before undertaking a journey;
the restless race of a traveler's heart before the journey begins

Admit your loss. What you are hunting tempers
underground—it's fool's gold

in the mining towns. The subconscious

is a shaft of broken tamarack for the graves
of miners. Be something the cage unlocks, monstrous

horizon. Hunt for X in the flumes

you've named salvation. Imagination is an act
of self-preservation. What tastes blue hot, is tough to catch

and impossible to open? Struggle. Try saving

anything save yourself. You were a child once. You read
Bradbury in the sluicing heat and the trumpet flowers

regaling the open fields. The subconscious is a dog.

o

Hello, I am lost. Which way to escape this heat, this
plunging? I clipped the ladder below

sea level, foam-green and barnacled. Lost

hot deflowering light. Or cave-
dwelling calypso, *Hello!* I am the open-

hearted end of a fool. The hunting dogs have lost

their trail. They're roiling in flowerbeds
and muddying your best hopes.

What's lost to your earth? They bury.

An Editor Advised Me to Stop Writing
Mother Bird Poems

The kitchen of my past smells of carne adovada
and green chiles blackened on the comal.
These days, I don't even like to boil eggs for fear
I'll overcook them—the whites will ooze
through cracked shells streaming into grungy
water I've forgotten to salt. My family could
eat peanut butter sandwiches for dinner every night
without complaint. I sit down to write
but what's the point? No matter how many beautiful stories
I create, some man whose uncle raped his mother
will snatch a young boy from the sidewalk
while he walks home, his mama waiting two blocks away
for his cowboy hat to turn the corner. But the hat
never comes and the boy she nursed and sang
Twinkle Star over and over while pouring bathwater
to soothe his fear of No More Tears
because even those burn—that boy who learned
to read by memorizing all the books at bedtime
but never would eat anything green not
smothered in barbecue sauce. Gone.
We vow never to let our children walk alone
but then my boy will run ahead in the mall
and I'll lose him. It won't matter how many poems
or baths. Except it will, like peanut butter.
The boy on the street, his too-large cowboy boots
forever walking home toward his mama. His mama
forever on the porch, searching the skyline for a hat.

Mrs. Francis Na Kai at the Birthday Party

After Laura Gilpin's photograph in "The Enduring Navajo," 1961

You dignify the rocker, your younger children
barefoot at your skirt. Pearls secure your neck.

Your daughter stands guard from behind.

Mrs. Francis Na Kai of the woven blanket. Your boy
spoke in code. 1932 you are a snapshot with him.

The anthropologist said you *showed incredible
composure at a formal dinner you both attended, especially*

for someone who didn't speak a word of English.

What piñon smoke has eaten your hogan?
What boxed diorama, spectacled theater of WWII?

The red rock of your skin scorches
the photographer's lens. Laura earned this picture.

She saved your first boy once, gave him

vaccinations. Your boy who should've been standing
beside his dad. Where's he gone in this 1950 family portrait?

Your boy in whose place, an American Flag.

Ars Poetica after Baby Lyuba

Trying to hold you still means
waking a baby mammoth frozen in the tundra—

thick, your nested heart,

a red scarf against the whitegrey backdrop, our thousand
words for *snow*, but none of them fit—

Why must shallow banks thaw?

Sediment still cresting her throat, they named her
after Yuri's wife, *Lyuba*, "love" in Russian.

Yuri said when he first saw her, he thought she was
an elephant, an infant, and he was uneasy.

But then he realized what she was.

Untamable creature, breaking through extinction,
I couldn't give you up for anything,
your wooly body blanketed to mine come permafrost,

come reindeer hunter, discovering
how beautifully we'd survived, together, through ice.

Volver (Bride Price)

for Rahila Muska

I wanted to return the scent of late-
summer, avocados blackening on the branches
on the grass.

      All that I love tonight—
the azure monarch laboring toward milkweed,
our lungs expanding in the rains

after running hills at sunset,
canary-yellow of the eggs we'll fry come morning—
might be lost in the morning

if you look at the beauty of the world—
the teenage Afghan poet, girl who named herself
after a smile and called the only radio frequency

      for women, for poetry, for a way out,
girl whose brothers beat her for disgracing them with poems,
with free will, girl who burned

      herself in protest and sang her final poem
from the hospital, and sang her final poem

on the radio, and sang, before she died

I call. You're stone.

One day you'll look and find I'm gone—

but if you look at the ugliness of the world
(all that I love tonight, tonight might be lost)

you may find a kind of burning.

Fernweh (At Gorge Bridge, Taos NM)

"farsickness": being homesick for a place you've never been

Above curved light above flash flood above
stilled hearts I could fly hundreds of feet

above monsoon earth still cradled
in its still breathable air above storm-

clouds' gunmetal boats sailing above
the creation of the world, not as I learned

in childhood but as it must have really been
above lightning burning pink holes

the color of punch and stars above
like twinkling strobes, as if I've been invited

to this spectacular party and all around me
sleeping like children while godlike

their parents drink and sing above the daily
fringe and hover into night

these faces of strangers like the flushed
and ruddy faces of the stars above

I long to greet. Again, hello! I am a passerby
I am a survivor of the world

I am a feather unmoored from birdwing
caught in your astronomical

wind parade. Above sandstorm above
windstorm above storm of my own made song

I will live here awhile. I will not jump tonight.

First Light in Tahoe City

The firs slant toward what sustains them
and what burns them without rain

the way I leaned against you all those years

you brought me home drunk and
propped me on the toilet seat

my head nodding toward sleep, those blinking
white party lights

those sugar pine, those beetles in the bush

as now the years have washed us of each other
now the aspen in daybreak flutter against

morning, and morning catches their
skirts, pins them with light.

I've driven all night to see something that reminds me

of you. Now I'm here and the water
shakes its black and the water

pools its light,

it's like even the mountains gather
the strength to move on.

Reverse: Ten Years of Marriage

Faucet water ticks and hours drip
        from wall to sink, our drain
full with them, our entire mysterious lives.

You tell me of an optical experiment
        how our brains pattern dots to control
all that random.

            You've stopped breathing into my collarbone.
        You sleep on the couch though I've held
your place in bed.

The luck fountain smells of orange blossoms
        and wet copper pennies.
It requires these tokens

        of belief—(when will we fracture our belongings?).
We are sharp as umbrella ribs loose
        from their vinyl and poking haywire

into air, shiny lightning catcallers
        come and get me, I'm not afraid of you.
Breaking lends itself to surreality:

        bonefish growing hearts on the kitchen tile,
the hearts, bleating. Some of this makes sense
for we are creatures who long

and in our longing
connect star-patterns (in the dream, we made home
of meteors and our crashing

meant something) this decade
of wedding cake in its smoke-shade of hunger
tasting of campfire, metallic on the tongue.

I trace ventricles shaped like fish underwater
swimming backwards, where upstream
means splitting self from self

the way I wonder how lungfish
feel about deep space, that other separation.
I've asked for your lungs so I can breathe.

Reupholstering a Chair

You've become accustomed to ripping things
apart. What business do you have making
something solid? A chair is for support,
for resting at a table drinking black
tea spiked with honey whiskey. You could guest-
star on the home repair network. You could
survive the empty bed. Your love will no
longer unclog drains or screw in light bulbs
or replace the hydrangeas you've suffered
death in the tiny plot you vowed to protect.
You begin stapling but suspect you're missing
the point, your target, not pared wood
but bright blooms wounding the pattern.
Lie beneath the chair, lie on the cold
tile and see how the thing was made.

Snakes-Her-Skirt

Coatlicue, c. 1500, Mexica (Aztec), found on the SE edge
of Plaza mayor/Zocalo: basalt, 257 cm high
(National Museum of Anthropology, Mexico City)

I take Coatlicue with me to market,
　　　　her rattlesnakes striking each other
beneath her skirt, zoomorphized

feet, pieces of eyes and skulls, talons
　　　　and feathers, to help me find something
for the little love I've lost—

some dish some spice some poison—
　　　　until she frightens other shoppers
and we're asked to leave. Gravediggers

exhumed her once in 1790, with the sun stone,
　　　　but reburied her for she so terrified
her diggers. Hands and human hearts

around her neck, she's meant
　　　　for power and I can't bear myself
asking for something as mundane

as death. She's basalt heavy, tired of being
　　　　misunderstood—I drag her behind me
with a rope. Bound together

by those broken parts, she's decapitated
        (they say her children killed her)—they say
she swallows us who need her, allows us to live

in darkness. I lead her behind my empty house
        through the alley, small shoes strung on a telephone
wire, through the side gate toward the backyard

where my daughter used to pull
        the heads of dandelions and blow her wishes
into the chill night air. I offer Coatlicue

a beer from the ice chest, but those two snakes
        sprouting from the stump at her neck,
their split tongues curling downward,

decline. She pulls up a chair and pretends
        to rest, though we understand that's impossible.
She and the other mothers saved our very cosmos

by offering their own lives. I ask her would she let herself
        be turned to stone again for love,
that pain. She peels off her hand heart hand

necklace and offers it to me.
        I take it to the place my daughter lies, stone
to stone   and then I understand.

The First Time

like lukewarm tequila-
bellied worm
I broke candles to my skin
testing my wrists
for how wax would burn
how it could cool
in shapes around my catclaw
scars though I had no cat
no seeping teardrops tattooed
like the girls I envied
'cause they wouldn't fall
for a boy let a boy
take them to the country
for nothing for la henna
'cause I *was* falling and didn't
catch my own damn
dream where I could be
two people
in the truck bed of sweet alfalfa
I could've done more than say
in my mind
not the first time not ever
I didn't want to
the first time
like rain like fat
like blistering ink splotches
I was raped, wax like lips
mouthing *No*.

Curanderisma

Playing light as a feather   stiff as a board in the backyard
after curfew with the girls   we called ourselves witches
the crabgrass brown   summer drought scratching
my bare thighs, I lifted   the edges of girlhood
it peeled all the way   back like bark like scabs on knees

    I'm trying to explain   what happened (they return)
    the women buried   beneath alligator juniper, sage
    fringing desert   greener for fitful monsoons, even
    the sleeping sister   volcanoes cloak themselves
    in purple coneflowers   in yerba mansa and selfheal

en la curandera's jardín   I rub their planked bellies
their branch-limbs   as mama did when I came home
bruised, emptied, sallow-   mooned—the newspaper yellows
their faces, unnamed night   I wriggled through dirt
feathers in my mouth   the night he took me to drought-
dry fields, cracked skullcap   needling through rock
as edges of hearts find   holes for digging

    sana sana colita de rana   *si no sanas hoy sanas mañana*
    mama would sing me   before I grew rocks for babies—
    if a frog's tail falls off   another grows, if a frog's tail
    is chopped off or hides   underground, so wet this season
    the tadpoles believe   they're safe in the desert

I was never a murdered   woman but a witch
trying to make myself whole—

                              found me feathered, buried
beneath board, found   my bare body's fraud, found me
other in sod, I was never   a murdered woman until I lay
back flat and floated in air   like a cheap magic trick

turned me sheet turned me chains turned me saw box
for coffin for love

        (we believed in the game as girls)
the way we take   everything in, swallowing
water for air   healing for lemon balm

     for snake's tongue—

the garden asks for my hands   the garden asks nothing.

Junkyard Halflight

My boy wakes me in the night; his own
strange smell scares him. He's wet his bed again,

needs me to change his sheets, his clothes.
Our wounds, fish-colored in the dark,

ring the basin like leftover bathwater, my
children flapping in the tub, slick as seals.

I grew up too soon, smiling at boys vaguely
familiar. I spent two births. No, not spent.

Lent. What returns is this: floating. But later,
a dawn. Small things come back, in pieces.

That time of day I wasn't afraid to close
my eyes. The white flies weren't yet lured

by streetlamps; the air still held its damp menudo.
On one side of the house, the cemetery

where we buried the girl, her face
swollen with ditchwater; on the other side,

a landfill. Downwind, the swine barn where guys
took me nights, its smell of straw-piss webbed

with sex. It's not so strange my son's bad dreams
remind me of my own. He asks to sleep in my bed

so I lay a towel down. In his nightmares
he's drowning. I tell him they're just dreams

but he doesn't believe me.

Santiago's Song

When I was a boy, I longed to be transformed—
to be othered in the closets of my best friend's

sister, in her mother's high heels that almost
fit my own large feet, in the scarves and purses

in which I'd keep the hours like sparkling seashells
before my father and brothers rang the doorbell

and I'd quickly peel myself apart like a mermaid
slipping back into her fishtailed cover, relinquishing

those slender woman's legs, that resistance
to water. Driving through El Paso and the mesquite trees,

the jackalope I swore I saw leaping through
the yellow columbine like Texas gold, its impossible

antlers promising me breasts instead of Adam's
cursed apple, and on the radio *The Hanging Tree*—

I know the uncensored lyrics said a necklace of
rope—know they changed it to a string of hope

so I'd come to the tree, where a dead man
transformed his love and fled. When I was a boy

I wasn't a boy. When I was a mermaid, I was really
the sea. When I was in love, there wasn't a tree.

Safe

Jacklight to my back they've taken
my body the driver

the shooter the spotter
blurring my vision

to the wrangled border
dovetailing dirt

my head lobs floorboard
digs my jeans bone-handled

crotch like tissue paper
wadded to staunch the bleeding

          ○

    If a girl witnesses
          rising like God against a sweet acacia stand
herself

    who can hear the sound

she makes above the scrub of dust

          the waste of night?

Manju Speaks

*Rajasthan police were stunned when a marble miner
showed up at an outpost holding his daughter Manju's
bloody head in one hand and a sword in another.
Manju had been living with her parents after leaving
her husband. She was planning to elope.*

The blade did not slip, was not
a trick, a blood-baked flick.

That flanged head, that shocked black
hair that father carried through town

triumphant, his bulbous face
twisting, his dishonored sandals

clapping dirt—not
mine not mine not mine.

I didn't have a neck.
I didn't have a lover.

No wedding, ever. No demon father.
I belong to cloudskull, starfruit, dreamfog.

My ma's hands swallowed me back
in the field where she was late picking pulses.

Inca Ice Maiden, Momia Juanita

Peru procession to Ampato

I'm left to sleep in a cave of ice,
my belly full of brittle chocolate
and llama meat like the privileged,

like a queen, fattened of gold,
my hair roped in a hundred gangly braids.
There was no path up

the volcano but what the priest
had forged, weeks I knew I'd cross
realms, bearing messages

in the beads clotting my wrists, my neck
a wall of rock for my liana shawl,
and in my hands a clay hourglass

filled with maize beer for the gods.
Now you call it the rescue in the Andes—
what a mummy you've made of me

with your scientific minds, your
sympathies, your presidents catcalling
me from the land of beautifully fixed

living. You called me forgotten
till you dug me up, with my tiny sandal,
my bruised copper pot, my spiny

oyster shell. You tell children
how if I were alive today I'd be
in high school, reading Wuthering

Heights or Their Eyes Were Watching
God. But don't you see?
Mine still are   and the ice won't melt.

Earth

You knock my socks off. I mean
when I'm sitting on the grass

I need my feet bare, and the inchworms
mulling the dirt of me, of you, I've carried

in my pockets in my hair in my nails—
I've heard there's not enough of you

that soon I'll be through with you
or I'm covered in stuff we call dark

matter and the energy is pulling us through
emptiness. The reason I'm here

and you. From my balcony I hear
construction workers singing on a rooftop,

their hammers against wood, against nails.
I've felt Atlas carrying you

the way I've carried
love, the way I've carried my dead

and buried them back to you, inchworms
in the grass. I mean we're in the dark

here. I mean I'm holding us.

I Believed All Poets Were Dead

and that I'd be the only poet in the world.
I had no idea there were others
besides the Frosts and Dickinsons, never
heard of coffee houses or spoken

word. Where I grew up, we barreled
bonfires and burst kegs. Ended in ERs
for drunk-driving quads in the sand or trying
to keep up with the boys, drink for drink—

but I loved poetry, even if I didn't know
where it lived. Poetry tasted like the chile
con limón on the rim of the plastic beer cup,
smelled like alfalfa in the menudo pot.

I ate it with a knife. Though I met Frida—
she was a painter and she was dead.
Today at my scholarshipped writers' conference
the one Latina editor lifts her pointed Jimmy

Choos from beneath the speakers' panel
and says *I'm tired of reading about barefoot Latinas.*
All the Latinas I know wear shoes—
and they're fabulous shoes.

Easter Sunday

Mama's exercising to nuns praying rosary
on the Catholic channel, leglifts each Hail Mary,
lunges each Our Father, Dad's absorbed in
online conspiracy theories, and my kids are digging
backyard dirt a cat keeps pissing in.

Sunday brings a ready-glazed ham I can stick
in the oven. Browning sugar, droning nuns
and occasionally *the fucking government's bailing
out the banks again!* The cheese is crisping.

For the kids, I pass off the ham as bacon,
slicing pieces frying-pan thin. I begin carving
the rest, readying it for plates. We'll eat
at the table together again, with placemats.

Then I see it.
Spit it out! It's bad! I yell into the living room,
scooping the toxin from my family's mouths.
The entire bottom of our sweetly coated
Easter ham, green and molding.

You know that feeling of déjà vu?
How time decouples till we're split
from even ourselves. Sometimes we get stuck.

We've signed divorce papers. I've torn them up.

Sunday takes back the ham and gets a roasted chicken,
a bouquet of flowers, but I can't stomach

anything else. I wait for signs of illness,
the kids eating mac and cheese, Mama drinking a shake.
Dad pokes at the broccoli, shouting between bites
about those goddamn drones.

Sunday says *I can usually smell decay from a mile away.*
I can't stop crying.

Rehab

Mrs. Sheets at the rehab center
thinks my husband is The Angel of Death,

calls him Saint Sunday
and wails for him at night, waking

patients down the hall. *Some
wounds I cannot heal* he says

as we walk along the bosque
arguing about my lingering

in the past:
you can't let anyone or anything

go. I scrape my shoulder
on the rusted metal gate along

the canal, and begin to fear
I've contracted tetanus, which leads

to lockjaw. Mrs. Sheets
fears Jesus doesn't love her since

her affair and subsequent divorce. What's
crazy is the way I jumped into the water.

The way Sunday jumped
in after me. The way I revised the story.

He didn't jump. He didn't save me.
I only pretend, like Mrs. Sheets,

that saints should
carry us to redemption.

In the Shower with Sunday after Watching *Lost*

I panicked. I closed my eyes and I was
the shipwrecked woman who'd struggled ashore
to birth infant twins in the sand while
a woman already of the island
acted midwife long enough to pull
the screaming boys from the narrow canal
then murder their mother to steal them
for her own. I believed you capable of turning
smoke, turning monster. You might've needed
something of me I was not willing to give.
Shampoo stinging my eyes, you reached
to wash my face clear, but I flinched, then
slapped. It happens every time. You'd censor
my imagination if you didn't believe in love.

Sunday Night Shift

There's something about the dark
matter holding us together I can't stop imagining
as the skeleton of God, like we've found
meaning in the scaffolding, even if no heart,
mapping the bones of the ribcage, puzzle boxes
like shape sorters, a place where everything
fits. How often I feel alone, winter greening
into spring on the cottonwood outside my window
and the sky shading grays or blues, lighter
or darker for weather and earth's circling
dance around the sun. Does it matter the colors
are blind spots? One winter night the sky reflecting snow
I saw further into the city than any night before—
it was white with light, rooftops shining
as if we were living in a snow globe and the world
were still. It was a miracle, that light.
For hours you were skidding on the ice
and nearly couldn't make it up the hill toward home.
The nightshift was long, the ground thick with it
what allowed me, through darkness, to see.

Safe (One Boy)

Crossing the street outside his house
Aunt Lucy's firstborn black boy

died. If she'd been standing in the yard
watching him span the fifty yards to school

she would have seen his body
slammed to the ground, the guards

mistaking him for someone living.

A few years later as we walked home
from the grocery, a car in the crosswalk

hit me and my boy. The stroller rolled
like a tape recorder on repeat.

The boy given to me at birth
squeezed through his birthmama's legs

plum-packed crying and suctioned
his cone-shaped head sliding from her belly

hitting the pavement.

I tugged open the stroller straps
screaming *My baby*

screaming *whatthefuckdidyoudo?*
to the girl who'd been texting blind

in the haze of dusk
and C u L8r LOL.

But my boy was fine. His body
intact. His eye only purpling a bruise.

A few years later Trayvon Martin
went down to the corner store

for a Mountain Dew and a bag of Skittles.
You see where I'm going?

We slumped on the curb
rocking and rocking.

In the Emergency Room

The belief that we may finally encounter glory. A child screaming our only language for pain. The talk turns to heaven: two of them waiting for news, another trying to breathe and the wait long. The lit tunnel of my eyes like lightning bugs low in a summer field, so the sounds amplify: the heaven they discuss, throbbing my ears, underwater heartbeat. A painting Tanguy named *The Lovers*, whose salt bones, mineral deposits, curve-lined wishbones like so many parabolas on a piece of ocean-colored graph paper nearly puzzling together but not quite. Like anchors above the lovers, smaller pieces of bone floating in chaos, unconnected to any larger bodies. One perched like a woman's torso, another the head and horns of a white-skulled horse, and then one dancer's lithe arabesque, or grand finale. If heaven were a curtain, it'd be rising.

Abiyoyo

In the African story
the father is a magician with a wand and the son's
a musician playing his flute.

That trickster father
makes cups disappear so that drinks
splash on faces

or pants suspend mid-thigh and cups shatter
to packed dirt. They're sent away—
father and son, both outcasts.

Then a giant comes. At this point in the story
I'm thinking of how my child fell
from a fence and broke his wrists and

no one would help him. I mean, no one
was around to help. Or they'd fled the scene.
My boy. Limping home carrying his own hands

like dead fish at his arms.

Son and father lure the giant away
to the edge of the woods for it's a story.
In stories, giants disappear.

Father and son are welcomed back. As saviors are.

Sunday heard this story as song on Reading Rainbow
when he was a boy
and had no father, no flute, no magic wand.

He bandages our boy's wrists.
Shows him the scars on his own knees,
one in the shape of a hook, another, a crooked smile.

What were you running from, son?

In the Beginning

was a dead girl. In the helm of the grass-green
pickup. His body becoming her body

becoming a dead body becoming a flightless bird

                    thick and black without wings
whose head stuck into sand, whose heart
was buried as cactus flower
is buried in the beginning   (the sound

at the mouth of one who cannot love
but by stinging)

the flesh of a scorpion weed, the scent of citrus
bitter in the scorching trees, half-eaten

by night animals. Theirs is the smell of palms
damp around copper pennies—hers, of onions
rutted in ditches. She begins
        this way, the light still dark, still

whether the sky opens, girl opens,
the trees rustle open their skirts or the wolves
in their caves licking open their grayblack wounds

—her heart a rash on their pink bellies.

The beginning of night was this way
was chokecherry—
            her second self.

In the beginning
the swollen center of her

left wrist for in the beginning she carved
into her bright new body.

The Accusation

1.

Sunday pulls out the dictionary for our love
means *to blanch* one of us has said

to whiten something
by growing it in the dark.

Another counters *nigrescent is the process*
of becoming dark. Like night or wives stuffed with fear.

My man glanced at a singing girl.

When I was a girl. Have you ever misplaced
memories like painkillers in the throat of your purse?

When the police came I imagined a bucket.
I imagined fish swimming in this bucket

and my girlhood.
No witnesses. But the mother.

The police report says he climbed on a rock.
There was no rock.

2.

Heat rash prickling, we ate mangoes with chile,
scissors clipping butterfly wings in three

equal parts: fireflies the night our adopted
son came barreling through the teenage girl

who handed him to us. I was so jealous
but couldn't admit then anything but love.

Husband, staring into the gaping hole
of my throat, Chile Colorado and other trifles:

my bluing hands combing through your black braids
and from my mouth, a curse: *Cut them off.*

When the policeman came to my door
with the white woman: *Don't limp to the station,*

man, run, and *tell them your side of the story.*
Flies circled the pan dulce on the table.

3.

Bastard, watching a young girl in the shower.
I didn't know then how gorgeous and developed.

I'd only heard her voice. *Crazy Joe's daughter,*
I'd heard her screaming to her mother.

Send me away like Crazy Joe. I dipped
corn tortillas in oil, nestled them

in a glass skillet, red enchilada sauce in the beds
of my fingernails. Either you're innocent

or you're guilty. That's the long and short of it.
But your braids on the bathroom floor, and my hands

on the scissor blades, colorful wings, Folklorico skirts
in my Delilah grasp, dancing us to safety. Our boy

with caramel cheeks, with curls budding to kinks,
burning in the playpen, unsung and unchanged.

4.

I took the test and my data suggests
little to no automatic preference

between African and European
(Americans). I've always been a good

test taker, demon bubble-filler, whiz
with a fill-in-the-blank.

How I deal with pencil shavings, pointed
edges of leadless heads, pink thumbs

of erasure? Another story altogether.

Funk You Up

My boy and I in the car
to the courtroom, groovin

to Uptown Funk and my boy feelin
the downbeat the way in my gut

I feel when he asks about his birthtown
Detroit, his birthmama and the boy

at the party 'cause that's all we know
of his dad—   how it comes

to music (always) and we're laughing
hard in our bellies   but if you listen

to the lyrics? Girl
hit your hallelujah, girl hit

your hallelujah, this call-and-
response this backbeat

kid teaching me what he's learned
about breaking—   he broke

his wrists and didn't cry
but said of the x-rays *I'm broken!*

There was fire after the riots.
There was breaking when I was a girl

torn to hayfield, left to ditchwater.
I swore to Sunday *I'll fuck you up*

when a girl accused him and I believed
her.   Would my boy's birthmama

have done better—   kept him
safe? Girl

hit your hallelujah (call the police
and the fireman). Sunday

I'm in love I'm in love I'm
sorry.

Machine for Second Chances

Here we've tried blessing
the trauma, the fire to our skin
in which I've awoken crying *who held the matches*
into the matches of my hands.

What can I tell you? Love
held an iron's cord to our necks, balanced
us atop a chair, tied an end around a metal rod
wedged in a doorway. Here

there is bird noise. Here, a muted desert and a murder
of crows.

I've heard of a machine that makes
meaning, like stardust. I've heard of second
chances before siphoning back into primordial
nothing: the stars in our bodies, fastening themselves

to breathing machines and beating
machines and spinning firing synapse machines
the way everything is weightless on the inside
of an unmoving body far
from any other body

like in space, like in nothingness.

Hawking says even black holes
are not completely black—

Here snakes in scrub oak
rattling. Here petroglyphs, and climbing
the lava rock mountain and the footholds steep
and the footholds careless—here
we step into our life.

Elegy, for Sunday

Love in the stranger bed on Sunday
    rain undoes the day's sun
knowing what I know about you, love

in the heart of my bed
    (in the church of my body)
Sunday's the body's heart

any day I cannot warm your blood—

O love, blood, Sunday,
    where is your heart and the fat plums,
orange in the peels of the bed on Sunday?

You peel an orange and hand
    me a newspaper I'll never read for fear
of what I'll find.

It's Sunday, and there's death in the world
    and rain—

What's gone from the heart on Sunday,
    man in the flesh of the dead, or stranger,
it's Sunday every day till I believe.